You Are the Artist
of Your Life

Adria Firestone

StoneFire Press

To Ralph —

Warm Wishes, Adria 3/24/15

For information contact:
Adria Firestone
adria@adriafirestone.com

ISBN: 0983553777
ISBN-13: 978-0-9835537-7-9

Version 1.1

To my angels who guide me unfailingly,
no matter how much I protest;
I surrender.

Table of Contents

Acknowledgments

Steve Harrison, my generous mentor, I thank you.

Jack Canfield, my guide and wise man: yes, the principles work, if I work the principles!

Brendon Burchard, you could light a fire under a stone – and you did! Thank you.

To my EIC, Freddie, your patience and love is my rock.

Donna, my friend and fellow realist, your understanding of my journey is unique solace.

Teresita, my sister and refuge, I thank you with all my heart. You were there for the last word of this book and 40 years of shared lessons.

Darling Maddy, your love, your support and your magnificent questions enrich my life now and always.

Diane, the depth of your healing gifts have made my journey easier. Thank you.

To the teachers beside me from my birth, I thank you for the lessons both horrific and beautiful.

Introduction

May each experience I have gone through and each lesson I share help you find your way to your authentic self. I hope you see your beauty and humanity as you write your thoughts and transform your life.

Be loving and kind to yourself; you will show others how to treat you by doing that.

May my observations give you comfort, enlarge your understanding and help you grow into the shining beings you are already.

You truly *are* the artist of your life. Make it a masterpiece.

Adria

CHAPTER 1

When you don't know what to do, don't do anything

How many times in my life have I tried to *make* things happen? Almost always. And almost always, my attempts to muscle through have been abysmal failures.

I'm arrogant. I'm arrogant about my intelligence, about my ability to think on my feet and about my strength. I didn't realize how much harder it is to surrender control. My higher self, that space between my words and my thoughts, is where my real wisdom lies. That place is my connection to the divine spark we all possess. But I am impatient and I am afraid. I try to calm my anxiety by 'doing' instead of listening for guidance.

What you think is right for you may not happen in the way you want it to happen. You may not get what you want, but you will always get what you need.

Everything happens at the perfect time. It happens at the time when your karma and your soul are ready to handle a particular test. In the much larger picture, all things are fair and all is well.

You have choice. You can fight and struggle or wait for guidance.

I'm an impatient woman, and at every turn, life has compelled me to be patient.

It's your choice. When you don't know what to do…

What thoughts rise? Write them down.

CHAPTER 2

Regret is useless

Shoulda, woulda, coulda? A complete waste of time. I have done many things that hurt others. I did things that were unwise. I hurt myself. I did things that were just plain stupid. Does it help me or anyone if I stay stuck in that place of regret and self-blame?

I say *I'm sorry* with directness and with sincerity. It is not easy, but it is right. Those who raised me never apologized about anything. They taught me how much that hurts and how wrong that is. I chose to take that teaching to heart and be different from my teachers.

The past is something to be learned from and then discarded. We need to keep the lessons but not the pain. The regrets of the past will cripple your present and color your future unless you are willing to drag them out into the sunlight and heal them.

One day I realized I did the best I could with the knowledge I had at the time. It felt as though a huge burden had been lifted from my shoulders with that simple but profound realization. It came to me as I was writing my morning journal pages and in my meditation.

When I know better I will do better. Each day I'm alive and awake to my life, I am learning more.

Again, when I know better, I will do better.

What do you need to do to forgive yourself and let go of the past?

CHAPTER 3

You can't make anyone love you

How much I wanted my mother to love me. She told everyone she met how she never wanted a child. She would say this in front of me all the time. I accepted it as normal.

The fact is, she was so wounded she couldn't love anyone. That didn't make the ache or the desire go away, but when the yearning would rise up and threaten to strangle me, the reality of her pain calmed me down a little.

My father taught me to seduce anything you were afraid of. He was a master teacher. When you create an artificial situation, reality will eventually reveal it was just a seduction and not love. You can enchant someone for a few minutes, for a few hours, even for a couple of years. The work is exhausting: I have done it. You are on stage 24/7 and the rewards are not worth it. In the end, they still don't love you.

If you can't be who you are, you will never know the joy and freedom of being real. Authenticity is worth the hard work it takes to achieve. A relationship can thrive, in spite of obstacles, if it's based on truth and reality.

The snow goose need not make it self white. Neither need you do anything but be yourself.

~Lao Tzu

Are you trying to make someone love you? The person who is naturally right for you could be as close as the apartment next door.

CHAPTER 4

What is to give light must endure burning.
~ Viktor Frankl

When I first read *The Road Less Traveled* by M. Scott Peck, I hated his first three words but - life *is* difficult.

I believe each soul comes here with a purpose and it is our job to discover that purpose. If that is so, might our challenges be preparation for the job we are to fulfill? Suppose we are to influence many other souls and we had not been tested. Suppose we didn't know if we could really manage such a difficult task?

The tests that come to each soul may be small and petty or they may be huge like physical deformity, debilitating health issues, or mental limitation. You are not alone, the tests are for those around you as well and not only for you.

No matter the proving ground, it is a valuable arena for us to grow, to fulfill our purpose and to leave a positive imprint - if we have the strength and wisdom to do that.

You don't develop courage by being happy in your relationships every day. You develop it by surviving difficult times and challenging adversity.

~Epicurus

How have your trials and tests helped you? Write your thoughts on these pages. What has made you stronger?

CHAPTER 5

I am the artist of my life

I looked at my life and I didn't like what I saw. I didn't like the set, I hated the dialogue and the plot line sucked a big one. Then I realized, I wrote this disaster.

That could only mean one thing, if I'm the one who wrote it, then I have the power to change it. I can rewrite it.

That realization changed my life.

We humans think we are miraculous creations designed by some invisible power sitting on a throne in the vastness of the universe. What we forget is that we are a microcosm of the creator and as such, we are powerful creators as well.

As powerful creators, we have the ability to design our lives.

We can't control what life throws at us. But we have absolute control over how we react to what fate throws our way. I can choose my medium, my colors and my design because I am the artist of my life.

Everything you can imagine is real.

~Pablo Picasso

What don't you like about your life? What do you like? What are you grateful for? What do you want to change?

Pick up your brushes, your colors and create your unique design. Start now.

CHAPTER 6

The only person I have the right to change is myself

When I see someone going through a difficult time, I find solutions in my mind. I'm a natural problem solver. But it's not my responsibility to impose my solution on them.

I don't have the right to tell anyone what to do with their life. I can show them doorways, open windows, give suggestions, coach them and lead and inspire by example. Beyond that, I have no right to change anyone.

Once I realized that, my life became simpler and less burdensome. Everybody around me, I'm quite sure – breathed a sigh of relief. Giving up control is both scary and empowering.

My mate is perfectly who he is. If I don't like who he is, I shouldn't be with him. If his behavior changes and he suddenly becomes a thief, I have the right to say. "I will not tolerate this. Stop it or I am leaving." That's my choice and it's *his* choice to change his behavior or not.

If my boundaries are securely in place, I will have no problem asking for what is right for me. My responsibility is to ask for what I need and then make a decision based on whether or not those needs are met and how important they are to me.

A healthy, balanced relationship embodies compromise. But where does your compromise end and where do your boundaries begin? Answer those two questions and life will become so much easier. I promise.

CHAPTER 7

You miss 100% of the shots you never take.
~ Wayne Gretsky

When I was depressed, I didn't want to go anywhere, do anything and I certainly didn't want to risk anything. I had little enough as it is – at least that's how I felt. I couldn't see anything to be grateful for.

I stopped moving. I became stagnant. But I realized if I didn't risk anything, I would never know what was beyond my self-imposed barriers.

Was I afraid of failure? No, I already felt like a failure. My attitude was, if I try, nothing will work anyway, so why try? I was caught with no hope of breaking the cycle.

Like cats, we hate change. We may be in a difficult situation, but we get stuck in our uncomfortable comfort zone.

No one looking at me from the outside would have known what a fight it was just to get out of bed, just to pay the bills, just to go to work - it took superhuman effort to counter the inertia and sadness I felt.

Nothing will change if we don't change it. If we simply allow life to happen to us we give up not only our responsibility, but our freedom. When I realized my inaction was depriving me of my freedom, I began, with tiny baby steps, to take charge of my life again.

Take just one step - one tiny step. Take back your freedom. What small action can you take right now to break the stalemate of depression?

CHAPTER 8

Fall down seven times, get up eight

This martial arts motto gave me the strength for one more tiny step so many times. Not only can these words lead us out of our dark cave of despair, but depressed or not, this is the only way to get through life.

These words embody what mental toughness is for me. All of us are given tests. Life is never supremely easy.

I don't know anyone whose whole life is a joyous coasting downhill, happy as a lark and with all their needs taken care of. If there is someone out there like that, email me right now. Teach me.

I remember when I first went to Milano to study voice. I thought I spoke Italian because I'd studied it at the University. I was wrong. I felt isolated, alone and wondered what on earth I was doing there. I was the proverbial stranger in a strange land.

When the fear and sadness became overwhelming, I would help one of the sisters in the convent where I was living, to do some menial task.

In a flash, engrossed in helping someone else, I forgot my own sad loneliness. It works, try it.

Who can you help right now? What person or organization needs your energy? There is always someone lonelier and more in need than we are.

Ready, set, action.

CHAPTER 9

My habits determine my present and my future

Not taking care of myself was becoming a habit. It was getting downright scary. It was too much work to take a bath, too much work to fix myself nourishing food, too much work to comb my hair and too much work to clean the house. Life was too much work.

I realize now how fortunate I was to have a job to take me out of the house. If not, I think I would've completely deteriorated. The lack of self-care had become a habit.

I was taught I didn't deserve to care for myself because I wasn't worth very much. My only worth was being a glamorous showgirl. The effort was for my career, not for me. The treats were for my career, not for me. The pretty clothes were for my career, not for me.

Ten years into my sad state, I had planned to get my hair cut once I lost some weight. Nothing was changing and I decided to get my hair cut and colored anyway. My attitude about myself began to change. Weight began to drop. My habits began to change.

I encountered more problems that would've stopped me dead in my tracks. The first thing I wanted to do was cancel my hair appointment. A wise friend said, "Don't cancel it. You need to do this for yourself." True.

What small or symbolic thing will make you feel better? Go do it right now.

CHAPTER 10

Drop the idea of being someone, you are already a masterpiece. ~ Osho

I performed Bizet's opera, *Carmen* so many times. I loved the card reading scene in Act III. I began collecting tarot card decks. One of my favorites is by Osho.

There is an *Ordinariness* card in the deck. When I first received this card in a reading, I was horrified and my ego crushed.

Surely I'm not ordinary. Well, yes I am. It turns out, we are all ordinary and we all have special gifts, but we don't all have the same gifts. What a bore it would be if we did! Scene: I'm driving through the desert in a Lamborghini. I have an opera singer in the seat beside me. The car conks out. Who do I need: an opera singer or a magnificent mechanic?

Marianne Williamson in *A Return to Love* says:
We think we're more impressive when we put on airs. We're not of course; we're rather pathetic when we do that. Grandiosity is always a cover for despair.

I have never believed I was worthy, or that I was enough. I was taught otherwise and I believed and trusted those who taught me that sad lesson. That is what they believed about themselves as well. I'm still working on this lesson.

Keep working on self-worth. Don't give up. It will take time: you are worth that time and effort.

CHAPTER 11

It takes courage to grow up and become who you really are. ~ e e cummings

It takes guts to let your authentic self hang out, to drop all the grandiosity. The hardest thing I have ever done was to drop the definition of myself as an opera singer. A forty year habit is hard to break.

One of the first questions we ask when we meet someone is, "What do you do?" Isn't that a strange thing to ask somebody you don't know?

Our measuring stick of worth has to do with the role we play in society. What if I were to say to you, "I'm a trash collector." It's more glamorous to say I'm an opera singer and I travel the world, isn't it?

A trash collector gets paid better than an opera singer because the work is consistent. A sanitation engineer has benefits, retirement and a 401(k). A singer wears prettier clothes and the soundtrack is better.

If I didn't sing, the world continued to turn. If the sanitation engineers go on strike, try walking the streets of New York. Slight difference in actual and perceived power, yes?

Who is better? The opera singer or the trash collector? Neither. We are not measured by what we do for a living but by who we are as people.

Throw away the artificial measuring sticks and ask yourself *who am I* **and** *what do I offer?*

CHAPTER 12

I am the knight on the white horse I have been waiting for

I think most of us harbor a secret desire for a *deus ex machina* to come out of the sky and rescue us. It ain't gonna happen. We are the *god in the machine*. We have been given the power of choice and free will. We don't need to wait for anyone to rescue us.

My most cherished prize is my Carbonell Award for Best Actress in a Musical. I played hundreds of performances of *The Man of La Mancha* with fantastic leading men (John Raitt, David Holliday, Ed Ames, Harve Presnell). In retrospect, I realize I wasn't Dulcinea, I was Don Quixote!

I tilted at windmills, saw beauty where there was none and held a vision of the world that didn't match reality.

Now I know I have the power to create the world I imagine. I have the power of discernment; I can see the monsters. I can walk around them. I have the freedom to create a life I love.

Don't wait another second for anyone to rescue you. Put on the costume of yourself and jump on your white horse – even if it's only to take your dog for a walk.

See the monsters for who they are, don't waste your energy on them. Walk away from the energy vampires.

Grab your coloring book and design your world your way.

CHAPTER 13

The truth will stand up when everything else falls down. ~Paul Cook

Lying is hard work. Telling the truth is even more difficult. In the end, the truth is simpler – you don't have to remember what you said. I used to embroider the truth to make myself more likable. It's not worth it. I also used to protect people from the truth. That's not my responsibility.

I don't mean when you find out something you must immediately run to a person and blurt it out. Instead, take time and listen to your instincts. You may need to give them a gentle hint. You may need to keep your mouth shut. All of us are on our own path, on our own time line. You may lose a friend by telling them the truth. Maybe they were your friend or maybe it was time for the friendship to end.

With enormous compassion, I asked my best friend (she was 45) who had a burning passion to be a singer, why focus so much energy on something that was causing her so much pain and was not fulfilling to her? She had sung one small role in her life and acted in a couple of plays. If you don't sing, you are not a singer. If you don't write, you are not a writer, etc. The 15 year friendship ended and she told me she had always been jealous of me.

Who needs to hear your truth? Why? The people who don't wish you well will fall away. As you reveal who you truly are, your circle of friends will change. That's a good thing.

CHAPTER 14

Karma is fair

What I send out returns to me. It may not be from the same source, but it comes back at me like a boomerang. There is so much in my life that simply doesn't make intellectual sense. The more I study, the more I explore religions, philosophies and pathways, the more I believe reincarnation and karma exist.

The fact that life is difficult and not fair is reality, but if we accept it on a deeper level, it's all fair. We get exactly what we give.

When I consider what I would like for myself, although it may have a different form and shape for someone else, I desire positive things. Aren't those desires the perfect blueprint for action?

Suppose in past lifetimes we abused power? I witnessed my father in this lifetime misuse his spirituality, his charisma, his intelligence and his sexuality to control others. It made me very afraid of my own power. I'm past that now but it took a lot of hard work to get here.

There is an inherent balance in life. Nothing you do goes unnoticed. While I don't believe there is an old bearded man sitting on a throne watching over us, I think our souls know what is right and wrong.

If you get quiet and listen, all the guidance you will ever need is right there in that silence. Take ten minutes every day and rest in the space between your thoughts. Write down what floats to the surface.

CHAPTER 15

Everything you want is on the other side of your fear

I admit it. I'm a scaredy-cat. I get all excited about what I want, and then don't follow through to get there. Why? Because I'm afraid I might fail or, I might succeed and my life will change. Does that sound familiar to you?

Les Brown the motivational speaker says, "The reason most of us aren't living our dreams is because we're living our fear."

How do you get around fear? Actually, I don't think there is a way around it or over it. The only way to conquer fear is to walk straight through it.

Courage is not a lack of fear. Courage is walking on in spite of fear.

When we are afraid to make mistakes, we limit our success. I remember even in my voice lessons, I wanted to do such a good job, it became a performance instead of a lesson. I deprived myself of making mistakes and didn't get the full value of my lesson.

I have failed a lot in my life; it's part of life. We are all here to learn. There is something in the American psyche that teaches us it's a crime to fail. Our competitive sports are all about winning. Sports figures constantly dishonor themselves just to have the word *winning* before their name.

It's okay to fail. What failures have you had? Look at them now. Have they been useful in any way?

CHAPTER 16

Let someone else be right for a change

Have you ever realized what hard work it is always being right? Move over and let somebody else be right.

It used to matter very much to me to be right. Maddy, my adopted mother and father all rolled into one, gave me excellent advice about relationship. Whenever you get into a disagreement, always ask yourself if it is more important to be right or to be happy.

Those are wise words. Although I mess up often, I try with all my heart to keep that counsel.

But what about truth? Truth, beauty and contact lenses are all in the eye of the beholder. We all see things differently and interpret things differently. As long as you are comfortable with your own integrity, you won't need to fight for the supremacy of being right.

When you are congruent with who you are, with the words you speak and with the actions you take, there will be no need to prove your superiority in any way. You will come to a place of peace and power that is astounding in its quiet depth.

Work on being your authentic self. Work on making your words and actions congruent - a reflection of your shining soul.

In what ways can you let go of being right?

A truly powerful person has nothing to prove.

CHAPTER 17

Choose your battles

Another way of saying this is, get your priorities straight. Does it really matter that someone doesn't load the dishwasher according to almighty you? Or is the priority to have clean dishes at the end of the cycle?

Isn't it too bad that the China-plate-Aunt-Tilly-gave-you-but-you-never-used-but– didn't–give–away–because–it–would– hurt–her–feelings–even–though–she– has–been– dead – for – 10 – years, got broken? No. One less thing to dust.

In the movie *Evening*, there is a moment when Lila Ross, (Meryl Streep) visits Ann Lord (Vanessa Redgrave). After seeing her dying friend, she says, "We are mysterious creatures aren't we? At the end, so much of it turns out not to matter."

We take ourselves so seriously. We fight about things that, in the end, have no importance. Choose to see what really matters. Choose to spend time with a friend who needs you. Choose to share your heart and your time with the people who matter in your life. Do you think it's important if dust bunnies roll under the furniture, or if your car is washed?

We come into this world naked and leave it the same way. The treasures we share, and the *only* ones we keep, are the souls we touch and the love we share. Pick your battles, prioritize.

What really matters to you? Are you honoring those values with your time and attention? In what way?

CHAPTER 18

Surrender is not defeat

Most people think surrender is sitting in a dejected heap waving a white flag. That isn't surrender to me. Surrender is having the guts to release control of a situation. I don't mean releasing responsibility, I mean releasing control. I admit it's scary, but the rewards are tremendous.

Because of my fear, I love to control situations. I find that if in my meditation I get quiet and listen for guidance and then follow that guidance, I am much better off. When I try to manipulate things intellectually or *make* something happen, instead of allowing it to unfold naturally, I'm getting in the way of my own angels who are there to help me.

It takes far more courage to trust your instincts and allow something to happen instead of making it happen.

Trusting our instincts comes naturally to us as children. Later in life that gets drummed out of us and we are instead controlled by arbitrary rules. This is what you *should* do, this is what you *must* do. Says who?

Start finding ways in your life in which you can surrender. Where can you let go of control and allow things to unfold?

This will take practice. Have patience with yourself.

You didn't develop the control habit overnight. You won't be able to get rid of it overnight.

CHAPTER 19

Love is all there is. ~The Beatles

The most powerful energy on this planet is love. I'm talking about big love. Maybe big love is just another word for compassion. It's the kind of love that allows your heart to melt over an adorable puppy's antics or be more tolerant in life.

That same love, if you allow yourself to connect to it on a daily basis (it takes practice) will allow you to look at someone making an ass of themselves and feel compassion. It's big love that allows us to turn the other cheek, not the demands of religious martyrdom, but the realization that we, too, have behaved stupidly. Compassion is what allows us to repay cruelty with kindness.

The challenge of trying to live this way is not easy. Ironically, my motivation was anger at being treated so badly by those who were my trusted caregivers. When they treated me disrespectfully, I treated them with respect. When they were cowardly, I faced them with courage. When they were cruel, I dug down deep into my fury and came up with kindness.

I was determined I was going to beat them at their own game. It worked. One day when I was about forty years old I realized I had grown into the strong being I had only pretended to be.

How can you better face the difficulties of your life with compassion for others, and most of all, for yourself?

It will take practice, have patience. It's worth it.

CHAPTER 20

Be kind, you can change someone's life in an instant

If you suspended your negative judgment, do you realize how different your life would be? Suddenly, without even trying, you will be infinitely kinder to everyone you meet.

If we stop judging everything as good or bad we will be more fully in the present, and will react more authentically to the souls who cross our path.

I think of kindness as love in action. A kind gesture can be a lifesaver for someone in despair. Kindness does not have to be big. It just needs to be present. Kindness can be as small as looking into a stranger's eyes and smiling. Drop the insulation of being *cool* and instead show your humanity.

Don't forget that no matter how wealthy or poor, brilliant or simple, alone or together, we all want to be appreciated and valued. We each have the power to hold the space for appreciation and the time to value another.

Andy Rooney said, "The average dog is a nicer person than the average person." Isn't the thing we value most about a dog that they appreciate and accept us, if we are worthy or not? They simply love us.

Extend your kindness and see people melt under your warmth. Your life will become easier and smoother. What has changed?

Try being consciously kind for an entire day. How do you feel at the end of the day?

CHAPTER 21

Drop perfection, it's not your job

Perfection is one of the greatest blocks to success I know of. Why not instead of perfection, be in competition with yourself and strive for personal excellence?

There will always be people better than you are; there will always be those worse than you are. That is why the only authentic measure of your success or failure is your competition with yourself.

The release of trying to be perfect took such a huge weight off of my heart. I replaced striving for perfection with personal excellence. Excellence is one of my mantras. The excellence I strive for is to be better than I was five minutes ago.

When you can truly say to yourself, I have done my best, you will feel enormous peace. It is impossible to do more than your best.

Your best will vary from day to day and week to week, as you feel differently. No matter how you feel, do your best. You are releasing yourself to be all you can be.

Let go of being perfect and adopt instead, doing the very best you can every day with the energy and knowledge you have at that moment.

Remember, when you know more, you will do better.

Always do your best and you will find new power and serenity. Have you done your best today?

CHAPTER 22

Acknowledge your feelings

I was taught my feelings, my wishes and my thoughts were unimportant. I was taught anything I wanted was selfish. For the longest time, I never knew what I felt. I had suppressed my feelings completely and become an expert at filtering everything through my intellect.

It was very difficult for me to acknowledge my feelings. I had to get help. It was a process, a long one. If you have been pushing down your feelings for most of your life, you're not going to be able to uncover them instantly. Give yourself all the time you need. Time is infinite.

You may be horrified to find you are filled with fury, pain, and negative emotions. That's okay. You need to process all of that. You will, I assure you, get to the other side. When that happens, your perspective will change and your view of life as well.

Debbie Ford's book, *The Dark Side of the Light Chasers* is perfect for beginning to unearth all of these buried feelings. Anything that is unacknowledged in us will control us unconsciously.

Get help and drag those feelings into the light. If when you are reading about these feelings, your first instinct is to say *oh no, that's not me* – I say, mark the spot and return to it. There is something you need to look at.

Get started on this work as soon as possible. It will completely transform your life.

CHAPTER 23

Respect yourself

"Don't take yourself so goddamn seriously." This is an exact quote of *Rule Number Six* by the former conductor of the Boston Philharmonic, Benjamin Zander.

Taking yourself lightly and with humor is part of the formula. You are not infallible. You will make mistakes. We are as clumsy and as magnificent as tiny kittens. We are humans animated by a divine spark.

The practice of becoming impeccable with our word, self-respect and honor is the foundation of your life.

Your word matters. It's all you have. When you promise something, keep the promise. Be attentive to what you say. Words can heal and words can wound. If you become respectful of every word you utter, it will color every relationship in your life.

You can embody these values with practice. Your life will become simpler and your decisions easier. When you fully accept the consequences of your actions and your words, your relationships become stronger and easier.

Start now. Don't wait. Your word is a binding contract. Consider your words and consider their effect. What contracts have you made today?

Connect to your true feelings and allow them to surface. Speak them with care and compassion.

As you honor and respect yourself, you will give others the same respect. Your life will bring you, and others, much joy.

CHAPTER 24

You cannot give what you do not have

Because I was raised by needy-greedy people, I did everything in my power to be the opposite. I was extremely generous. Later in life, I realized I had no more to give. I had no reserves. I'm not only talking about things, I'm talking about emotional reserves as well.

I put myself in a position of giving instead of receiving. I viewed it as more powerful. It's also a way of avoiding the lesson of being able to receive. I began to notice no one gave me anything.

If you saw a magnificent knight riding around on a white charger, armor blazing in the sun, would you ask him if he needed anything?

In reality, a knight in full armor needs a squire to get him in and out of his armor and get him up on, and off of, his horse. So, anyone who appears strong and invincible needed help to get that way. Think of the ways in which you need help.

Most of us are like that knight in shining armor. We have strength and vulnerability living side-by-side. For us to be able to share, we need allies and resources.

I want to feed the world. Will I feed the world any faster or better if I starve myself?

What have you done in the past day, or the past week to build up your emotional, physical and financial stores?

CHAPTER 25

Trust yourself

As a possession of narcissistic parents, I have issues with trust. Yes, the choice of the word possession instead of child is deliberate. I have worked on my issues and have achieved healing, but the work never stops.

The largest shift occurred when I realized I didn't need to force myself to trust others. What I needed to learn was how to trust myself.

I have learned I am a survivor. I have enormous strength and resilience. I have learned I have mental toughness: I don't give up easily.

I have learned that no matter what anyone does to me, I am fast and resilient enough to defend myself when needed and grounded enough in self-love that my action toward that person will simply be defense and not retaliation. War does not create peace.

Along with trusting myself, I have learned the importance of widening my boundaries so I feel safe within the space I need for serene living.

What have you learned about self-trust? Ask yourself these questions.

- What boundaries do I need to lay down to feel safe?
- How can I shift from trusting others to trusting myself?
- In what ways can I increase my comfort zone?

CHAPTER 26

The only constant is change

Like the weather, everything in our lives changes moment to moment. Nothing on this earth is forever, that is reality.

Do you dislike what's happening in your life right now? If you do nothing, and simply wait, eventually it will change. But do you want life to *happen* to you? Or would you rather be a participant in your journey?

Think of how different your life could be if you choose to take the reins in your own hands and decide on the pace, the path and the purpose.

If you want to meet your friend in San Diego on Wednesday at 2 PM, you have to know several things so you can make arrangements to be there on the appointed day at the appointed time.

Where will you begin your trip? Florida? Los Angeles?

Are you flying there? Driving? Train? Are you hitchhiking?

All of these variables will cause you to choose a different time frame to arrive on the time and day you have agreed upon.

Make some definite plans about your future. Create steps to achieve those plans, but hold them loosely.

If you do absolutely nothing and wait for change, are you happy with what might happen? What would you do differently?

CHAPTER 27

Say what you mean, mean what you say

In spite of the diplomacy we have learned or the social lies we have been taught, try saying exactly what you mean for a change – always with compassion.

Honor the power of your word. When you say something, even as small as, "I will meet you at 4 o'clock," are you aware you have created a contract? Honor your contracts and your life will change. Yes, I am saying this again. It is essential.

When the people in your life realize you honor and respect your word, they will become more responsible with their own words.

Our words and our thoughts create our lives.

The practice of Zen asks you to be mindful of everything you say and do. Pay attention, with lightness and detached observation, to the responsibility of creating your life.

Pay attention to your self-talk. Pay attention to the words you use when you ask for something. Pay attention to the verbal contracts you create.

If you don't like what you observe, you have the choice and the power to change it.

What sort of a life are you designing? What contracts have you made un-consciously? Consciously?

CHAPTER 28

The tiniest light dispels darkness

Have you ever been in a darkened theater? There is an inky blackness that descends when every single light is off. If you light one tiny candle, the light dispels the darkness.

Our lives are exactly the same. There are times when we are convinced (I have been there!) that all is lost and things will never get better. One good thing about that point in your life is, the only way out - is up.

One tiny spark can illuminate a new path, a new way of doing something or a need to surrender everything you thought was true and start over. Is that scary? You bet it is.

This may be the time for you to embrace the fact you have no answers to any of the questions you thought were even remotely important.

A breakdown can become a breakthrough. We come to this world filled with optimism, clarity and an easy willingness to ask for what we need. We are tamed by society. We lose our spontaneity and our connection to our deepest and highest selves. We lose our light, or learn to cover it for fear of offending others.

It is our Light that most frightens us, not our Darkness.
~Marianne Williamson, *Return to Love*

I dare you to sit in the dark for a time and feel the discomfort. Ask yourself, what is my light? What is my spark?

CHAPTER 29

Share

Have you noticed that sharing dispels fear? Think about how scared you are if you have to talk in front of people and prove to them how much you know. Think of how exciting it is instead to share something you love with others? The energy is totally different.

Sharing is also the comfort you feel when you share with a friend. The trouble you share is cut in half, the joy you share is doubled.

Nothing is really ours. We use things for a while and the joy is increased if we share them with others. When we share information, we are spreading education. When we share our resources, we are spreading wealth. When we share our point of view and our dreams, we are sharing our humanity.

Very few of us, as we age, continue sharing our dreams. If the dream is past, hold on to the beauty; I think it's a way of staying young in attitude. We need to honor and share the milestones of our lives. We need to celebrate and mark with ceremony the occasions of our lives.

You staying at home all alone on New Year's Eve?
Unthinkable...The countdown should be shared with someone,
or it's just another set of numbers passing you by.
~E. A. Bucchianeri, Brushstrokes of a Gadfly

Don't wait another minute, share something of yourself today. Share a smile, a meal, a warm embrace, but share yourself. Your joy will be multiplied. What will you share?

CHAPTER 30

Forgive

No one in my family ever forgave anyone. I, too, learned not to forgive. I finally realized not forgiving someone was like swallowing poison and hoping the other person would die. It doesn't work. The only one I was hurting was myself.

I don't believe we need to forget we were harmed by someone, but neither do we need to dwell on it. We must find strength to release the pain and keep only the lesson.

When you begin to understand the discomfort and unhappiness of the person who has harmed you and feel the beginnings of compassion, you are on your way to forgiveness.

Think of the people you have yet to forgive. Go through a process of trying to see things from their point of view.

Release those who have harmed you and place them in a mirrored bubble so that every negative thought they send out is reflected back to them.

If you can't think of a good reason to forgive someone, how is this?

Always forgive your enemies; nothing annoys them so much.

~ Oscar Wilde

What people in your life do you need to forgive? What pain do you need to release? What can you learn from the pain that has been inflicted on you?

Keep the lesson, let go of the pain.

Forgive yourself and everyone else who needs it.

CHAPTER 31

Serve

*E*verybody can be great…Because anybody can serve. You
don't have to have a college degree to serve. You don't have
to make your subject and verb agree to serve. You only need
a heart full of grace. A soul generated by love.
~Martin Luther King Jr.

My life changed the moment I realized rather than teaching my
students what I knew, I needed to ask first, how may I serve? My
approach changed. My students' grasp of my subject changed.

The minute we let go of our own self-importance, fear drops
away and we are transformed into childlike beings longing to share
what we love. That is one of the most effective ways to get rid of
the paralysis of inaction in our lives.

When we serve, we release our desire to prove how important
or how skilled we are. Instead we become excited to share what we
know. Think of this. If you are teaching a child you love your
favorite song, are you worried about whether they will like your
voice or not? No, you are sharing what you love.

When you ask how may I serve, you release yourself from your
inner critic's nagging, you free your creative self, and you give
yourself the gift of touching someone else's life.

**At the end of your life, it's not how much you have earned,
how much education you have gleaned or how many awards
you have won. Your worth is in the imprint of the souls you
have touched. Who have you touched?**

CHAPTER 32

Listen

When we listen instead of talk we receive valuable messages from our surroundings, sometimes from the most unexpected sources.

I was in NY's Port Authority very late one night waiting for a bus when I saw a disheveled drunk shambling unsteadily in my direction. Inside of myself, I said, "Oh no, I sure hope he doesn't come and talk to me." I buried myself in my book.

He walked right up to me, bent down and put his face close to mine. "Thhhose men, yuh know, those men aren't treating yuh right. Get ridda anybody who ain't treatin' yuh right. Yuh deserve a lot more."

He gathered himself together and kept ambling. At the time, I was struggling with a divorce. His words were a message from the angels.

Listen with your eyes. Listen with your ears, and most of all, listen with your heart. When we're in a conversation, we are formulating our reply to whatever the person who is talking to us has said. We're not really listening.

Develop your listening skills. Try this experiment. Stop multitasking. When someone talks to you, whether it be on the phone or in person, truly focus on them and listen.

Do you find yourself getting more out of the conversation? How is your interaction with others improving? Start listening. You will be surprised at what you hear.

CHAPTER 33

Be grateful

As I was raised by people who saw nothing but lack in their lives, I didn't understand what gratitude was. I always looked at my life in terms of what was missing.

Over years of intense self-work, I began to shift my perspective. I began to understand the attitude of gratitude could transform my life.

If I change the way I look at things, the things I look at change. Quantum physics proves this. Perception is everything.

Every time I light a stick of incense in the morning, I say thank you. Make a ceremony of *thank you*. It's fun.

Be thankful for what you have and you will end up having more.
If you concentrate on what you don't have, you will never,
ever have enough.
~ Oprah

Again, like anything else, developing an attitude of gratitude requires making it a habit. A habit requires practice.

Start noticing things that make you smile. Notice when some small thing you do or say makes another happy. Replace your negative self-talk with silent *thank yous*.

Get into the attitude of gratitude and not only will you change yourself, but the world around you as well.

What can you do to add to the quality of your life and the lives of others? Share the bounty of yourself. How can you show appreciation for everyday miracles?

CHAPTER 34

Accept what is

This has been one of my hardest lessons. So many times in my life I have pretended a situation was not as it was. I have fallen in love with emotionally unavailable men time and again. Reality tells me they will never be able to give me what I need. If I desire change, I must do the internal work and remove my rose-colored glasses.

How many times in my life have I seen the shining heart of a person who has been unkind? I *always* do. I do, because it's part of who I am and it's part of my purpose. We all have beautiful hearts and shining souls, even though our actions may not always reflect that.

I was around eight years old when I cut this quote by George Elliot out of a newspaper. "I want not only to be loved, but to be told I am loved...The realm of silence is large enough beyond the grave." I found it many years later when I was discarding things before I moved to Italy. The yellowed fragment was taped inside my toy chest.

I need emotional availability like I need air. I have learned to respect my needs. It is torture for me to be with someone who cannot express what is in their heart. The cure: accept reality as it is and move on.

The first step in changing anything is seeing a situation or a person with clarity and love. Once we truly see, then we can begin to accept. Acceptance is your first step to a new life.

What is it in your life you need to accept as reality? What is it you don't want to see?

CHAPTER 35

Take care of yourself

You are the most important person in your life. Does that sound crazy or exceptionally selfish? Maybe not.

I know a mother will feed her hungry child before she feeds herself, but if she starves, it is likely her child will as well.

So how do we find balance? If we are able, we are responsible for taking care of the physical body that houses our soul. If we don't, we become sick, dependent on others and a misery to ourselves.

When we practice self-care we are practicing self-love. We are respecting ourselves and honoring the life purpose we are here to fulfill.

You have a great body. It is an intricate piece of technology and a sophisticated super-computer. It runs on peanuts and even regenerates itself. Your relationship with your body is one of the most important relationships you'll ever have. And since repairs are expensive and spare parts are hard to come by, it pays to make that relationship good.
~Steve Goodier

Pay attention to these words. As women, we have been taught to be care-givers. Care for yourself, body and soul. What can you do to take better care of yourself?

Put the oxygen mask on your own face first. Isn't your life and your family worth it?

CHAPTER 36

Faith

Faith is the bird that feels the light when the dawn is still dark.

~ Rabindranath Tagore

Faith is that indefinable energy that has kept me afloat and on this planet when all seemed lost. Whatever your belief or religion, faith is that precious connection to the divine spark we all possess.

It doesn't matter whether you believe in Buddha, Christ, Mohammed, Allah or any of the great teachers who have walked this earth. Faith is the living connection between all beings, no matter the color of your skin, the form of your religious practice, or the beliefs that guide your life.

Your faith is the link between all that animates you (*anima* is soul, from the Latin) and animates everything in the Universe. We are part of a magnificent whole.

For me, faith is love. Faith is the compassion that allows us to forgive, to surrender judgment, and to embrace even what we fear.

Give yourself the gift of stillness. Take time to connect with the faith that guides you. It doesn't have to have a name or any formality.

When you find that connection, you will discover a strength that is surprising. It can manifest itself as simply as viewing the glass as half full.

What is the spark that keeps you going? What are the fears that keep you awake, and what quiets those fears?

CHAPTER 37

Now is all we have

We think we have forever. Not so. The moments we have right now are all we've got. We don't know if we have tomorrow.

Now is the measure of our lives; this very moment.

A friend was all upset because one of her roommates had a great job interview and thought she was going to move out in less than 60 days. I told her not to worry about it. Nobody knew yet if she got the job. As it turns out, she didn't get the job and she isn't going to move.

Do you realize over half the things we worry about don't happen?

We eliminate so much anxiety and worry if we stay present.

I'm not saying we should never make plans. I am saying if we do make plans we, and the plans, need to be extremely flexible.

The secret of health for both mind and body is not to mourn for the past, not to worry about the future, or not to anticipate troubles, but to live in the present moment wisely and earnestly.

~ Buddha

Meditation helps me stay present. What might work for you?

What can you do to remove the anxiety of what might happen? What tools will help you stay present?

CHAPTER 38

Nature heals

Before you run to your doctor and ask for a prescription for what ails you, have you tried hugging a tree? Are you laughing at me? That's okay. I'm used to it.

There is something so healing about being in touch with nature, even in the midst of a bustling city. Think about this. Would Manhattan be livable or bearable without Central Park? Those trees and greenery are the lungs of that huge metropolis.

Give yourself permission to sit and watch seagulls as they fight for food, or ducks as they glide magically on the surface of a pond. When is the last time you took off your shoes, planted your feet on the earth and stretched your whole body toward the sun? I bet you haven't done that in a while.

I forget how much a brief contact with nature refreshes my spirit, changes my perspective and gives me new power to keep moving forward. Don't ignore such an obvious source of comfort and inspiration.

Your frazzled mind can be calmed by watching a line of ants shoulder their incredible burdens and march in an orderly fashion toward their objective. Have you seen a hawk riding the air currents in lazy circles?

Get up right now and walk outside. Look at the sky. Feel that natural vitamin D penetrate your skin. Give yourself the refreshment of looking at clouds. What are you going to do to refresh yourself on a regular basis? Nature is available 24/7.

CHAPTER 39

Sex is not love

Sex is an exquisite seed that can *possibly* grow into love. All the literature and music of the world are about the sexual excitement of the first six months of love or about the ending of a love affair. Not much is written about real love and the hard work it entails.

Sex is that breathless excitement that makes us feel wildly attracted to someone, and allows us to fall in love with ourselves. There is no guarantee it will work or the attraction will last more than 24 hours.

How often we are dismayed when our sexual fantasies don't lead to happily ever after. The fact is, most of the time they don't.

Enjoy the beauty of sexual energy between consenting partners, but don't fool yourself into thinking its love.

Love takes time, a lot of hard work, compromise, respect, and above all communication, to have a chance of growing into that magnificent thing called love.

Take time and allow the beautiful, breathless energy of sexual attraction to either become a magnificent memory or the beginning of time spent together, mutual respect and the magic of partnership.

Are you confusing sex with love? Have you gone past enchantment to something deeper?

CHAPTER 40

Never stop learning

If you spread your elbows and don't touch wood (you are not in a coffin) you still have more to learn. A friend of mine made me laugh when he said that. It's absolutely true. It seems to me the purpose of being on this planet is to learn.

Curiosity killed a cat, but satisfaction brought her back. Be curious about your life, about others, about the *why* of things. Be curious even when you don't get answers.

Thoreau said, "Only that day dawns to which we are fully awake." Be awake and alive to your life. You will find if you have simple curiosity, you will never be stuck in life-deadening boredom.

Give yourself the challenge of learning one new thing every day. It could be a new word or a new way of doing something.

Living intensely means being open to the miraculous, the beauty and the ugliness of life.

Live as if you were to die tomorrow.
Learn as if you were to live forever.
~Mahatma Gandhi

Play a game with yourself. Each day promise yourself you will learn one little thing that's new. Write it down in your morning pages. How has it changed your life - even in the tiniest way?

Share what you have learned with others. We are all teachers and perhaps more importantly, we are all students.

CHAPTER 41

Be still every day

I rarely find stillness in others. We are obsessed with our phones and our technology. I love and use all my technology, it enhances my life. But we have lost contact with the magical place between our thoughts where all the power and guidance we need is waiting to be accessed.

My life has changed since I added meditation to my morning mix. As recommended in *The Artist's Way*, I write my morning pages and take time to simply be still and allow my mind to be blank.

How different the day is when I connect to my deepest self. Sometimes it doesn't feel deep at all. Sometimes it just feels silly, but I still do it.

I am able to meet the challenges of every day with more equanimity and peace. I am more tolerant of the difficulties I encounter. My creative powers are more available to me when I meditate.

Give yourself a gift and get into the habit. Buy a timer and start with ten minutes. If that seems too long, start with five. Morning, noon or evening, what works for you?

Add journaling to the time. You don't have to write anything profound. Sometimes it helps to simply clear out extraneous thoughts. I know we're all busy. Get up earlier or go to bed a little later.

It will change your day - and with practice, change your life. It changed mine. What's your plan?

CHAPTER 42

Let go

Our family didn't have much money, but I had a few things I really loved. I had a huge stuffed animal, an orange donkey given to me by a dear friend and a tattered bunny. They were my faithful companions. One day I came home and they were gone. My mother told me they were dust collectors and she had given them away.

Over a year later I found them at a friend's house. I burst into tears when I walked into her room. She offered them to me, but I couldn't find it in my heart to take them back. This happened so many times. Although horrific lessons, my mother taught me to hold even what I treasured, with open hands.

The things we think we possess are not really ours. We are custodians of our possessions for a short time on this earth. My mother's greed and jealousy taught me to be generous and loving.

I have learned to give of what I have. The most important gift I can give is to hold a space of love for every being that crosses my path. That is a gift no one can steal and no matter how often you give it, it is inexhaustible and replenishes itself.

What gifts do you have to give? What things are you not using that could become someone else's treasure? Pass them on.

Create space in your life by clearing away the old and unnecessary. Start with one room, one drawer. Make space for new dreams and new vision. Let go.

CHAPTER 43

Say yes

When I was sitting at the bottom of my well of depression, my answer to everything was, *no*. I had no desire to do anything, go anywhere or meet anybody. I had no energy to share with others and no desire to reveal my wounded underbelly.

A long while after I began my intense self-work, I felt a tiny spark of change. I made a deal with myself. Even before someone finished a question, "Adria, do you want…?" My answer needed to be, yes!

Was it difficult? Oh my, yes. That first *yes* was a gargantuan task. But I did it. And little by little, I constructed a ladder out of my objections and climbed out of my sadness. I was afraid of anti-depressants and needed to take other measures. I didn't want to dull my pain or mask my symptoms but uncover and heal the source.

As with anything we have a desire to do, especially when it's something new, we need to give ourselves permission and incentive to change our stuckness.

What is it you want to change? Where are you stuck in your life? What actions can you take right now to begin climbing out of your inertia?

Remember, all the answers you need are in the quiet space between your thoughts.

Give yourself time.

You will find a way out.

CHAPTER 44

Get help

The more intelligent and strong we are, the more difficult it is to ask for help.

Sad thing is, once we ask, the professional we find may be a predator, as I found out. I ran for my life after a world of damage. I found another professional who when I needed time off from the intense feelings that were rising, asked me, "But what about me?" My perfect answer was, "For the first time in my life, this is all about *me*. It's not about you."

No matter what it takes, have the patience and the fortitude to find the right professional to help you. Interview your counselor, ask questions. Find a person on the same wavelength who has the skill and patience to explain the patterns in the pain they observe.

I found a psychotherapist who was also a life coach like me, and I made huge progress with this remarkable woman in a very short time.

Then I discovered EMDR, the most helpful therapy I have ever encountered. It was created for Vietnam Veterans and PTSD. It includes the kinesthetic, along with the verbal and it's so much faster than lying on a couch for five years – not my speed, financially or emotionally.

Get help. Find the therapy and the therapist that is right for you. This is an art, not an exact science. Have patience, ask questions and get recommendations. You *will* find your healing partner.

CHAPTER 45

Ask for what you want

In relationships, at work, in friendships and in love, we seem to forget our partner doesn't have a crystal ball!

I used to whine and moan that my relationships never worked out until I realized I had never revealed who I truly was. If I never show you who I really am, am I truly interacting with you? No.

When we are dismayed and sing our sad little song:

Nobody loves me,
Everybody hates me,
I've gotta eat a worm . . .

We forget we didn't ask for what we wanted. We go through life asking for what we think we can get, instead of asking for what we truly want.

Can you realistically expect other people to be mind readers? Can you expect them to get it when you drop veiled hints? Is there a difference between, I'll be here for a half hour, hoping someone will call you or, I'll be here for a half hour. Call me and we can talk. Which is clearer?

It was so hard for me to learn this, but so worth it. My life is changing because I ask for what I want now. I don't always get it, but there's a much better chance of receiving when you ask, isn't there?

Open your heart and ask yourself, "What do I want?"
Next, open your mouth and ask for it!

CHAPTER 46

I am 100% responsible for my life and my choices

Once we accept the truthfulness of this statement, we are on our way to designing a life we love and want. The fact is, we are the ones responsible for the choices we make.

It is true that life and events happen to us and many of them are life-altering. The thing we forget is, we have choice in how to *respond* to what happens to us. We can sit in a corner and bemoan our fate. We can curse a blue streak, stamp our feet or go for a five-mile run. We can eat ourselves into comfort. I have done that. We can accept what has happened as it is and decide clearly and logically what we're going to do about it.

Isn't that last course of action more powerful?

I find, with practice, my ability to process and deal with the difficult moments in my life is becoming shorter and shorter. One of the phrases I love to use on myself is (delivered with a New Jersey accent) *Take both hands and get over yourself.* It works. It makes me laugh and I take action a lot sooner.

What minor and major things have happened to you lately that threw you for a loop? Is there a better way to handle what happened?

Challenge yourself to write down three to five quick solutions in your morning pages.

Pretend you're someone else looking at this difficult situation. See any new solutions?

CHAPTER 47

Move

Very shortly after I left the stage, I found myself hugely overweight. Depression kicked in and the last thing in the world I wanted to do was yoga or prepare healthy food. After I had been working on myself for a while, I made a conscious effort to begin moving.

The deal I made with myself was, even if it was walking up the steps in my house, I would do it with consciousness. That awareness made a difference and began my healing. Even when I bent to pick up something, I did so with intention and with attention. Instead of griping about the fact I couldn't afford a housekeeper, I used the opportunity to clean quickly, lightly and with Zen-like awareness. I got each floor down to 19 minutes. I was playing a game with myself; that made it a lot more fun.

Even when I showered, I paid more attention to scrubbing my back, to bending down and scrubbing my feet. Turning a little more, I scrubbed my elbows and washed my hair. Just these tiny movements so delighted my physical body. All these small movements created a desire to do yoga again. I began with only one exercise per day.

Can you do that? Can you simply ramp up your movements during the day? What's your plan?

Make how you move pleasant. Part of the secret is to pay attention to *the feeling* of the movement.

Enjoy the everyday movements of your body. Life will begin to change, one step at a time.

CHAPTER 48

Sing

Have you ever caught yourself humming a little tuneless song? Or singing along to the radio at the top of your lungs and not caring whether anyone thinks you're crazy in the car next to you?

Singing is a remarkably healing thing. When you sing, or whistle, you breathe more deeply. Breath is the key to life. When you breathe more deeply (most of the time we don't) haven't you noticed you feel more energized, your metabolism gets revved up and you feel better?

Try this. When you are working on a project and get stuck, get up from the desk and just bend over. Do this often when you spend long hours at a desk. Let your arms hang down, let your head fall and feel your spine open up. Allow your fingers to get heavy. Allow your neck to get longer. Feel the weight of your head while you increase your bend at the waist.

Straighten up slowly, stacking each vertebra one on top of the other and take a deep belly breath. Feel your belly pop out when you breathe in.

Then just give yourself one minute of humming, making noises, singing a song. Drink a glass of water and go back to your desk. The whole world will look different.

A bird doesn't sing for applause. A bird sings because it has a song.

What is your song?

CHAPTER 49

Listen to music

About ten years into my career I realized with surprise I had stopped listening to music. Because music was my life and it was part of my work, I had stopped playing music. How sad.

Music saved my life as a child. No matter how my mother yelled at me or harangued me about the 'things' I had to do, I would lose myself in music and dance. I pretended to be onstage singing show tunes or opera. Because she valued me as a possible star, my mother allowed that.

My escape became my vocation, but in the process, I lost a very real joy in my life. My joy become my work and my work had become my joy. I learned music as fast as I could for the next job.

When I was deep in depression, the last thing I wanted was to listen to music. I didn't sing a note for five years. Literally, the music left my life.

I bought myself an inexpensive portable CD player/radio combo and put it in my office. I gathered my collection of CDs from downstairs and put them on my shelf in the office. Little by little, I began listening to all kinds of music again. In spite of myself and the fact that I was still deep in my own personal pity party, I began to feel better.

Can you do that? Add more music to your life. Listen to music that pleases you. Listen to every kind of music. What will you listen to?

Experiment. With each note you will find your heart lifting.

CHAPTER 50

Poor me

Pity parties are great - for the short term. When they go on for very long, it's time to change your tune. We have all felt despair. We have all felt the problems of our life were too much to bear.

Does it help when we wail and gnash our teeth? I actually saw my adorable little grandmother try to bite her elbows in full-blown Italianate rage (you had to be there).

Honor your process. Honor your feelings, mourn your loss and hurt and get on with life.

The acknowledgement of how you feel is vitally important because acceptance of your present reality is the first step to new clarity. From that new perspective you can take action to transform your present.

If I were given the opportunity to present a gift to the next generation, it would be the ability for each individual to learn to laugh at himself.

~ Charles M. Schultz

So, what are your steps?
- Acknowledge your feelings
- Throw a pity party
- Take a break and laugh
- Create a new vision/goal
- Get going

About the author

Adria Firestone walked out of an award-winning, international career as a singer and actor. Her credits range from Bizet's *Carmen* to *Family Guy*. She hit fifty years old and crashed into burnout and depression. It took her ten years to find her way out.

To learn, she became a teacher. To truly listen, she became a life coach. She broke through the shadow of childhood abuse and into real magic – she fell in love – with her authentic self.

That is how the book and program, *You Are the Artist of Your Life* was created.

Adria is the author of five books, a contemporary philosopher and a riveting speaker.

http://adriafirestone.com
http://youaretheartistofyourlife.com

Made in the USA
Charleston, SC
07 July 2014